3 THEORIES OF EVERYTHING

3 THEORIES OF EVERYTHING

ELLIS POTTER

Destinée Media

© 2012 ELLIS POTTER

Without limiting the rights under copyright reserved above, no part of this publication may be reproduced, stored in, or introduced into a retrieval system, or transmitted in any form or by any means (electronic, mechanical, photocopying, or otherwise), without the prior written permission from the publisher, except where permitted by law, and except in the case of brief quotations embodied in critical articles and reviews. For information, write: info@destineemedia.com

Reasonable care has been taken to trace original sources and copyright holders for any quotations appearing in this book. Should any attribution be found to be incorrect or incomplete, the publisher welcomes written documentation supporting correction for subsequent printing.

Published by: Destinée Media
www.destineemedia.com

Chief editor: Peco Gaskovski
Design, typography: Katharine Wolff
Inside diagrams: Ellis Potter
Sketch of the author: Andrzej Bednarczyk

All rights reserved by the author.
ISBN 978-1-938367-04-5

INTRODUCTION

THE FIRST CIRCLE
    The New Age Movement
    Experiencing Oneness
    The Cycle of Life
    Meditation and Language
    The Nothing of Zen

THE SECOND CIRCLE

THE THIRD CIRCLE
    The Problem of Opposites
    Humpty Dumpty

    Falling in Love on a Bridge
    Defying Gravity
    Change, Time, and Eternity
    Me and We
    You Gotta Serve Somebody
    Look, Daddy, Look!

    A Black Hole in the Heart
    The Solution
    To Put it Simply

45 QUESTIONS
    Themes for discussion
    with responses by Ellis Potter

For
Mary
my
wife

○　○　○

WHEN I WAS A BOY I asked the kinds of questions that many children ask. Children want to know how far is far, how small is small. They especially want to know *why?* I never grew up. I am still asking these questions, absolute questions, about life itself. I want to know what reality looks like when you think down to the bottom and out to the edges. I want to know what things mean in the final and absolute context. It can be difficult to ponder absolute questions because they can challenge our deepest beliefs. They can be threatening. But it's exciting to ask absolute questions. I believe it's healthy. I hope that if any of you have grown up that you will go back to being a child.

Small children start off with the hope and trust that reality makes sense. They believe that Mommy and Daddy are omniscient—a belief that is smashed sometime in childhood. It turns out to be like Santa Claus. By the time they are adults, most people have lost their hope and trust about how everything fits together. Their concept of reality shrinks to a narrow cultural viewpoint, to self-protection and control, or to indifference. They live in a smaller reality because the big reality, the absolute reality, is too difficult.

An absolute is a category that is so big that everything fits inside and nothing is left over. The category of *absolute reality* includes everything in existence. It's a theory of everything. Many people think there aren't any absolutes and they say 'there are absolutely no absolutes.' There is, however, a problem with this statement, because if it's absolutely true, then it must be absolutely false.

I believe the existence of absolutes is most likely, but is inconvenient and disagreeable to our egos. People nowadays are often motivated *not* to believe in absolutes, because if there are true absolutes, then we are responsible to the absolute. If there are true absolutes outside ourselves, then we don't invent ourselves. On the other hand, if there are no absolutes, we are free. We invent ourselves, and the meaning of everything is our reaction to it. This idea is obviously quite attractive. It also means we can stop asking questions.

But some people keep asking. They want to know what life is really about. What does it all mean? They want the truth. They don't want to just 'fit in' with their culture or believe what their parents taught them. They want to know what is real and actual, and they don't care what it turns out to be like. If it's meaningless and dead, so be it. If it's purposeful and glorious, so be it. And so they keep asking questions right to the bottom and out to the edges of reality, hoping to reach the truth, the *absolute* Truth—whether there is hope in it or not.

The Three Circles

When I looked for absolutes, I discovered there weren't many. I believe it comes down to three: Monism, Dualism, and Trinitarianism. They are quite different, but they do have some things in common, not least of which is the suffix *-ism*. *-Ism* means that whatever comes in front of the suffix *-ism* is the center of reality and the measure of everything. If science is the measure of everything, you have *scientism*. If the human being is the measure of everything, you have *humanism*. In terms of worldviews, there is *one-ism*, *two-ism*, and *three-ism*.

The most important thing these three worldviews have in common is their view of the history of reality. They each understand that there was a perfect beginning and then something went wrong, so that we now live in a situation that is not the way it was intended to be. We suffer. We are alienated. We worry. We feel confused. We want things to be made right again. Is there anybody who has never complained about how things are in the world? Very few people believe everything is perfect in the world, and most of them are either pretending, deluded, or never read the news. I believe it's normal to complain about things because things are obviously not right. It's understandable that people want things to be made right again.

The Western tradition of thought recognizes that the idea 'things were once perfect and need to be made right again' is the biblical view of history. In the beginning, a perfect God made a perfect creation and perfect people, and then something went wrong. There was rebellion, sin, and egotism. As a result, things are not right and we suffer, and we look for things to be made right again in Christ. This movement expressed in abstract terms is:

perfect—imperfect—perfect

Or better yet:
home—away—home again

In other words, it's a pattern of homecoming, of being away on a journey and returning to the place where you started, usually in a transformed way. You see this pattern in great stories, such as Homer's *Odyssey*, and you hear it in most music, whether in simple folk songs or in the *aba* pattern of the Viennese sonata form. Music and stories are so powerful because they are microcosms of the basic structure of the universe.

Now, if we recognize that things are not right, an important question is: What was reality like when it was perfect? If we know the answer, then we can have a better idea of what is wrong and what we can do about it. If we don't know the answer, then we can only say 'Ouch, I hurt.' Do you remember René Descartes? Descartes said, 'I think, therefore I am.' But I prefer to say 'I *hurt*, therefore I am.' I think that's closer to our experience.

There's an apocryphal account about Descartes. He went into a bar one day and ordered a beer. After he finished the beer the bartender asked, 'Do you want another one?' Descartes replied, 'Oh, I think not,'—and he disappeared.

But I doubt we would vanish if we stopped thinking. We would still exist. We would still feel. We would continue to suffer. There are people in the world who actually seek out painful experiences so that they can feel alive. They cut themselves and pierce themselves with razors and needles because it makes them feel like they exist. This is not a good solution to the problem of suffering, but we can sympathize with the desperation and appreciate the hint of truth behind it. In an imperfect world being alive and feeling pain are interwoven. They are tied up like a knot. Is there any way to untie this knot? Is there such a thing as existence without pain? What is the solution to the problem of suffering?

Monism, Dualism, and Trinitarianism all agree that reality was perfect in the beginning, but they disagree about the nature of that perfection, the causes of suffering, and what it means to recover the original perfection. Each worldview, in other words, offers a unique solution, a unique hope, to the problem of suffering. We can represent Monism, Dualism, and Trinitarianism by showing a circle in three different ways.

THE FIRST CIRCLE

Let's begin with Monism. Monism is not the same as monotheism. Monotheism is the belief in one God, but Monism is the belief in one *One*, a total unity that is the ground of everything. That is very different. If you believe in one God, then you have God and *not* God, but if you believe in one *One*, then you have only unity, or *All is One*.

Monism is an ancient worldview. It probably came about when people looked around at the world and felt a strong sense of unity. There is one earth, one sky, one sun, one moon, one human race, one cycle of day and night, one cycle of four seasons. At the same time, people saw diversity. They saw differences. The unities they witnessed were stable and dependable, but the diversities they witnessed were unstable and undependable. Monism argues that the original perfection is a perfect, changeless, eternal unity. We suffer because we have forgotten this original unity and live in an illusion of diversity. This illusion may seem very real to us, but it's an illusion nevertheless. According to Monism, the solution to suffering is to remember and realize the perfect unity again.

Monism is a central idea behind the New Age movement. Have you heard of the New Age? It's actually getting a little old at this point. The New Age came into popular thought about fifty years ago, in the time of the hippies, and draws some of its inspiration from astrology. There are twelve houses in the astrological zodiac, and history moves from one house to another like the numbers around a clock. We are now moving from the Age of Pisces, symbolized by two fish moving in opposite directions, to the Age of Aquarius, the Water Bearer, where all things flow together. We are moving from the age of opposition to the age of flowing together, and when everything flows together there is an increase in peace and tolerance, and the realization that all is One.

All is One! is the bumper sticker of the New Age movement. It's the great sound bite, the great evangelistic cry. *All is One.* If all is One, then you are God. You are the sun and the moon and the Milky Way and the whole universe. If all is One, then when you drink from a cup of water, you are God putting God into God. 'All is One' is so attractive because if everything is one, no one is going to disagree with anyone, no one will fight, no one will misunderstand, and no one will be lonely. All problems are solved if everything is one. You might sort of like this idea. If all is one, however, then you are me, and that might not be so attractive. If everything is one, relationships are evil because you only have relationships when you have the illusion of diversity. If everything is one, hatred is evil because hatred is a relationship, and love is also evil because love is a relationship.

Some people are inclined to protest against this line of reasoning because they don't want to give up the idea of love or relationship. But Monism is an absolute worldview that encompasses everything, and so you can't pick and choose to keep some parts of reality diverse or separate. Everything is one. Nothing is left out, nothing is divided, and everything is absolutely unified.

The New Age Elephant

A popular New Age story that symbolizes the idea that *All is One* is the story of the elephant. The elephant is a symbol of absolute truth, and humans are represented as blind people trying to discover that truth by touching the elephant. To me, it makes sense that the story involves a truth-*elephant* rather than, say, a truth-*bunny rabbit*. A rabbit is something you can wrap your arms around. An elephant is too big; you can't contain it and know it. The absolute truth, in other words, is *bigger* than I am. It's also reasonable that the people are blind because we are all blind in some ways.

In the story, the first blind person finds the tail of the elephant and says, 'Ah, the elephant is like a rope.' The next blind person finds a leg and says, 'No, the elephant is like a tree.' The third blind person finds the nose and says, 'No, no, the elephant is like a hose.' The fourth one comes to the side and says, 'No, no, the elephant is like a wall.' There is only one elephant, but the people have very different experiences of the elephant.

The elephant is too big for them to embrace and experience in totality, so they are confronted with a choice. One choice is to believe in the validity of one's own experience of the elephant, and—believing that all the others are wrong—argue, fight, and kill each other. The other choice is to respect each other's faith journeys and realize that *all* experiences are experiences of the elephant, and so we should live together in peace and tolerance. Which is the better choice?

Maybe you feel caught. On the one hand, you don't want to say that everyone's concept of truth is equally true, but on the other hand you don't want to say that we should argue and fight and kill each other. Actually, I once told the story in the United States and a young man put up his hand and said, 'Kill each other.' There is a certain honest logic in this reaction, but most people (even most Americans) would not think it was the best solution.

You can see by the way the elephant story is framed that it leaves you stuck, with no real alternative but to agree with the conclusion that everybody has a little piece of the truth, and nobody's piece is any more valid than anybody else's piece. But is there anything wrong with the elephant? When I ask this question during my talks, people usually focus on problems with the blind people. They may point out that the people don't pool their experiences, or that they are blind, or that they are small. These might certainly be problems, but what about the elephant?

Notice that the people in the story are active and communicative, but the elephant is not. He is passive and silent. He is available, he doesn't hide, but he doesn't come to the people who are hungering to find out about him. You see, in the elephant story, the absolute truth—the elephant—is less complex than the particulars—the people. But is this reasonable? Is this what we would expect of the absolute truth? What do you think?

Another New Age story that expresses the idea that all is One involves a drop of water. A drop of water has many problems. It is lonely. It worries about evaporation. It is frustrated because the function of water is for fish to swim in, but the drop of water is too small for anybody to swim in. The solution to its problem is to go back into the ocean and to become one with the all. Then the drop of water laughs at evaporation and is never lonely and the fish swim in it. This is how enlightenment is taught to children.

Experiencing Oneness

The idea that all is One has its roots in ancient versions of Monism. It is the foundation of Hinduism and Buddhism, the great monistic religions. The founder of Buddhism was Siddhartha Gautama. He meditated under the Bo tree for forty days and forty nights, and then he was enlightened. He opened his eyes and saw the planet Venus on the horizon. He knew he was enlightened, because he knew he was looking at himself. If all is One, I am the planet Venus. If all is One, you are God.

When I was a teenager doing Yoga and Buddhist meditation I had an unforgettable experience one afternoon. I experienced being the exact same size as the entire universe. The experience lasted about fifteen minutes and was very intense, although it could not have been very transformative or else it would not have become a mere memory. For the deeply enlightened person this experience is a constant reality.

There are many different forms of Buddhism, and people in the Western world are generally fascinated by them. Often, however, I believe we learn the surface details about something like Buddhism without going down into the basic principles of it. I don't want to talk about the details here. I want to focus on the basic principles.

In Buddhism there are four spiritual laws, called *The Four Noble Truths*. The first noble truth is *the law of suffering*. The law of suffering is that everything suffers. Everybody, whether they are from the East or West, can agree with that.

The second noble truth is *the law of the cause of suffering*. The cause of suffering is desire. If you desire, you suffer. You are not at peace. Desire is caused by relationships. For instance, if I meet with you, if I speak with you, I desire that you will like me and understand me. But you might not. As a result, I suffer—maybe not terribly, but I do. But it's actually worse than that, because even if you *do* like me and *do* understand me, I will desire to keep being liked and keep being understood, and so I never really escape the desire or the suffering that it causes. According to Buddhism, every form of desire—whether to be liked, or to be rich, or to be smart, or to be beautiful—causes suffering.

The third noble truth is *the law of the stopping of suffering through the stopping of desire*. Let me give you an example of what this means. If I have a toothache, and I desire that the pain will stop, and it does not stop, I suffer. But if I have a toothache, and I do *not* desire that the pain will stop, and it does not stop, I do not suffer. I am free. You see, the pain is there, but if I realize that I *am* the pain, I don't suffer. My experience is not *I have pain*, but *Pain is*.

The fourth noble truth is an eight-step therapy program to accomplish the goal of stopping desire. The program has a special name, *the Eightfold Path*. Are you familiar with the twelve-step program of Alcoholics Anonymous for overcoming alcoholism? You may have heard of other step programs that lead to health and coping with various difficulties. The Eightfold Path that the Buddha came up with is probably the original step program. Notice also that *fold* is a better word than *step*. If you have steps, then you leave step one when you are on step two, but if you have folds, like folds in a piece of paper, your progress keeps adding and building on itself, until you have all eight folds.

The Eightfold Path begins with practical things, like the right way of seeing things, right thought or purpose, right action, right speech, right way of earning a living, right effort, right mindfulness, right concentration, and then it adds larger parts of reality like the supernatural, the awareness and consciousness, and then meditation and Buddha-consciousness. In her book, called *Three Ways of Asian Wisdom*, Nancy Wilson Ross describes the process like this: First, you must see clearly what is wrong. Then you must decide to be cured. Then you must act and speak so as to aim at being cured. Your livelihood must not interfere with your therapy. Your therapy must go forward steadily, as fast as possible, but not too fast. You must think about it constantly, and learn to contemplate with a deep mind.

The Cycle of Life

Realizing the absolute unity of all reality is a long process. Many people soon discover that it's not reasonable to expect that in your lifetime you would manage the whole process. At this point the doctrine of *reincarnation* becomes necessary. Reincarnation is the idea that after we die we are born into another life on earth, live again, die again, and then get reincarnated all over again. As we do, we work through our *karma*. Karma is like a law of cause and effect. Whatever we do in our lives produces effects that need to be re-balanced, and this re-balancing often occurs in another lifetime. For example, if we murder somebody in one lifetime, then in the next lifetime we ourselves might be murdered, or maybe we might devote ourselves to saving lives.

Reincarnation can go on for thousands of lifetimes. In the West we tend to regard it optimistically, maybe because we're positive by nature. We think, 'Ah, you get another chance! That's good! Maybe I'll be born a king next time!' But in Asia reincarnation is not regarded as a blessing. It's more like a curse to be born into a life of suffering over and over. The goal of Buddhism and also Hinduism is not to be reincarnated but to *stop* being reincarnated.

When a Christian tells Buddhists or Hindus that they need to be *born again* they will reply, 'Oh, I know—and again and again!' Being born again doesn't sound like good news to a Buddhist or Hindu.

There is a word that Buddhists and Hindus use to describe the illusion of reality. It is *maya*. Being caught in maya is like being stuck in a bad dream. The dream is painful, frightening, and uncomfortable, but it's not real. What is the solution to a bad dream? You wake up. Awakening is the true realization of reality. It's also called *enlightenment*. It's waking from the nightmare of diversity and into the full realization of perfect unity. That is the gospel of Monism. That is the salvation of Monism. It's powerful, absolute, and deeply inviting. As a former Buddhist monk I can still appreciate this worldview and the strong attraction of it.

Meditation and Language

Methods are required to move toward salvation in Buddhism, Hinduism, and other Monist religions. The main method is called *meditation*. In the West, people sometimes think that meditation is concentrated thought. This is not what it means in the East. Rather, meditation is a method for the *stopping* of thought. Thinking must stop because thinking is analytic and relational. Thinking keeps us trapped in the web of maya, in the illusion of difference and diversity. It prevents us from realizing that if all is One then there are no relationships.There is only perfect unity.

Meditation doesn't have an agenda or logic about it. It is *being*. If you have a goal, you have a relationship with that goal. Meditation helps us not to have the goal but to *be* the goal. There are various ways of meditating, and many of them are quite therapeutic. If you follow various meditation practices regularly, you will feel more relaxed and focused, your stress levels will go down, your blood pressure will go down, the alpha waves in your brain will increase, your capacity to concentrate will increase, there will be more oxygen in your blood, your need for sleep may decrease, and you may live longer. Meditation is hard, but there are real benefits that come from it.

The people who practice it are not masochists. They are human beings like all other human beings. They want to be better and feel better. They want to make their lives better and healthier.

Aside from the practical benefits, the fundamental reason for practicing meditation is to achieve enlightenment. It takes many lifetimes to get to that point. Hinduism symbolizes the process of reincarnation as a wheel of birth and death that constantly turns—you are born into suffering and then you die, and then you are born into suffering and then you die. The purpose of meditation is to free yourself from the constant turning of this wheel.

Now, you don't become free by flying off the edge of the wheel, but by coming into the center. *Centering* is very important in meditation. Think about the center of a wheel or a car or bike. What is it? It is the axle. What is the center of the axle? It is a point. And what is a point? It is nothing. Even in physical reality, in the center of the center of the center, in between the molecules and atoms and gluons and electrons and protons, is nothing. This nothing does not turn with the wheel. The nothing is free from the turning. When you reach this absolute nothing through your meditation you also realize the absolute everything. You have achieved absolute freedom. You are fully enlightened. You become everything when you become nothing.

One of the most common methods of meditation is *mantra*. Mantra involves the repetition of words that have a meaning, first repeating them aloud and then internally. With enough repetition, they become a vibration and transcend their meaning. They become finer and finer until you are vibrating along with every atom in the universe. All physical matter vibrates as electrons change orbits. When you realize that vibration, you unite your self with all physical matter in the cosmos, and you become one with the all. This idea is where the New Age movement gets the concept of 'good vibes'. Good vibes are the vibrations of salvation, the vibrations of the unity in all reality. The use of mantra is not worship, even though religious words are sometimes chosen. Worship involves a relationship and functions in diversity. The goal of mantra is to be relieved of diversity and relationships and to realize the unity of all. For this reason, the goal of mantra meditation is to destroy language, because all language involves relationships among different things. You have to destroy language to be saved and to achieve total unity.

There are a variety of mantras. A simple one, and one of the most common, involves repetition of the word *AUM*. I remember chanting it in a monastery. When you do it, you breathe three times per minute. You empty your lungs completely and you fill them completely. When you really get going, there seems to be no motion. You don't know whether you're inhaling or exhaling. You don't know whether there is sound or silence. All becomes one.

When I give my talks, I usually perform one or two AUMs in order to give people an idea of what it sounds like. A philosophy professor once came to me afterward and said, 'I felt something inside of me when you did the AUM, something really big. I want to understand it.' I told him, 'You can't understand it. Understanding it means having a relationship with it, and that's not what AUM is about. AUM is about becoming one with AUM.'

The whole text is *aum mane padme hum*, which means *hail to the jewel in the lotus*. Lotus blossoms grow in the mud under the water, and propagate by shoots. Certain species have no seeds with a long stem and emerge through the surface of the water. If you see a statue of Buddha, look at the base and you will see little lotus blossom petals. It's the lotus throne, and he has lotus feet. It's a very important image for Buddhism. The lotus blossom has hundreds of petals. If you separate the petals and come into the center of the lotus blossom, what is there? Nothing. That is the jewel in the lotus. The imagery is beautiful and powerful. Buddhism may not be perfect, but it's not stupid or ugly.

A more complex mantra is *gate gate paragate parasamgate bodhi svaha*. The meaning is *gone, gone, gone beyond, gone beyond beyond, hail to the jewel in the lotus*. Repeat those words ten times every morning and your life will change. I can't tell you how it will change, but you will probably experience something. The poetry and symbolism are powerful. The words can still bring tears to my eyes when I hear them.

The Nothing of Zen

There are many kinds of Buddhism, such as Mahayana, Theravada, Tantric, Lamaistic, Nichiren Soshu, Pure Land School, and others. People from each kind of Buddhism will tell you 'our kind of Buddhism is the original true Buddhism.' We have the same situation in the West. There are many people who believe that God is a Lutheran, but we know He's a Baptist. Buddhists don't have problems that Christians don't have.

Earlier I said I am a former Buddhist monk, but actually I was a Zen Buddhist monk, and so I can tell you that Zen Buddhism *is* the original, true Buddhism. Zen really is special in some ways. The people who practice it believe in *Nothing*. They are not *Monists*, they are *Nonists*. But it's not a negative Nothing, it's a positive Nothing. Zen asks: If everything is reducible to One, then to what is the One reducible? This question is similar to the one posed by existential philosophers when they ask: Why is there anything? Why is there existence?

Zen doesn't answer the question with words and logical conclusions. It answers with an experiential realization. Let me try to give you some idea of the Nothing of Zen. You or I might say, 'It's possible that it will rain tonight.' This possibility is real and it's nothing.

You can't measure it, you can't weigh it, you can't know what color it is. It is nothing. In the same way, everything that is—every object, every thought, every emotion, every action—is possible. God is possible, the devil is possible, the earth is possible, you and I are possible—and all of these possibilities are nothing. Possibility is the mother of everything.

Possibility, here, is not the same as probability. Probability is something you can describe and measure. Possibility is not. One of the deepest truths of Buddhism is *Buddha is possibility*. In Sanskrit we say he is *Tathata*, or suchness, or undifferentiated quality. The Shakyamuni Siddhartha Gautama is called the *Tathagata*, which means *the incarnation of undifferentiated quality*.

I used to study with a Zen master. He is now over one hundred years old and still teaching. He wrote one book called *Buddha is the Center of Gravity*. It's a fitting title for a book about Zen. Every object has a center of gravity. Your body, a truck, a boat, a building—everything. But can you describe the center of gravity? What color is it? What shape is it? How much does it weigh? The center of gravity can't be described in such terms because it's only a theoretical point. In that sense, it's nothing. But it is essential. You can think of the Buddha as the essential nothing—or, to say it differently, as the essential central pregnant nothing.

In Zen, we say: If you see the Buddha, kill him. That means *if you have an idea that absolute reality is outside of yourself, you have to get rid of that idea.* You see, you cannot have any idea of the Buddha. You can't think of him as the fat guy painted gold in the Chinese restaurant. You can't think of him as one of the standing Buddhas or sitting Buddhas or lying Buddhas either, and not as one of the skinny Buddhas or young or old Buddhas. You must not see the Buddha. You must *be* the Buddha. And you must not *become* the Buddha, because you always *are* the Buddha. You must awaken and realize Buddha-nature. Then there is salvation.

I have given you a short Buddhist sermon. I don't know if any of you will be converted. I hope that you can understand the power and hope that underlies this worldview, and why healthy, intelligent people would devote themselves to it. They are not crazy. There are many lovely people who are committed to this idea of reality.

THE SECOND CIRCLE

Deakin

Not having really lived much in the second circle, I cannot truly give an insider's view of it. Although it has been very widely used as a theory of everything by many people in their thinking and believing, it is not as totally absolute as the first and third circles.

This circle, or at least a version of it, is known as the *umyang* in Korean. People from the West are usually more familiar with the Chinese terms *yin* and *yang*. Yin means *dark* and yang means *light,* and they symbolize the idea that absolute reality consists of opposites in harmony. You might also recognize this idea as connected with Taoism and Confucianism. It appears in other religions and philosophies as well, and is a good symbol for Dualism.

It's not hard to see how this view of reality may have come about. If we look around at the world, we observe many opposites in our experience of life: light–dark, hot–cold, hard–soft, pleasure–pain, sharp–dull, up–down, sweet–bitter, wet–dry, male–female. The idea behind Dualism is that life is good when opposites are in proper balance, or are in harmony with each other, but we suffer when there is imbalance or disharmony.

For example, if the weather is too dry, we suffer. If the weather is too wet, we suffer. If your personality is too outgoing, you suffer. If you are too withdrawn, you suffer. If we suffer because of imbalances, then the way of salvation, according to the second circle, is to restore the balance. The original perfection is a perfect balance or harmony of equal opposites.

Over the course of its history, the Dualist worldview has produced a number of therapies and practices to help accomplish balance in different areas of life, such as behavior, family and society, and past and present. The worship of ancestors is an example of the latter. Harmony is accomplished when living people, who exist in the present, give respect to dead people, who existed in the past. The same harmony can be accomplished when young people, who live more exclusively in the present, give respect to old people, who live more in the past. Also, younger people are stronger than older people, and the balance between the two is again brought into effect by respect—the stronger gives respect to the weaker. This kind of strategy may not always work out perfectly, but it can bring order to society.

Dualism has also influenced approaches to architecture and interior design through a system of aesthetics known as *feng shui*. To bring harmony to your living room, you might have a darker carpet to encourage yin energy, and bright walls to encourage yang energy. The overall result would be a balance of opposing energies and greater well-being to the people who spend time in that room.

Most of the strategies and therapeutic techniques of the second circle are probably effective to some extent. They make life better. They reduce suffering. They also produce different approaches in the case of health problems. In the West, our healthcare is typically based on pharmacology and surgery. This form of treatment is usually *against* something—against fever, against infection, against tumors, and so forth. In the East healthcare is often dietary and environmental and tries to bring the various elements in our body and its environment into harmony and balance with each other. Western healthcare concentrates on problem solving. Eastern healthcare concentrates on problem prevention. Both approaches to health can be effective—people from Asia don't live shorter lives or less healthy lives than people in the West—although sometimes the methods used in the East may seem strange or dubious to people who are not familiar with them. It might be good to combine the wisdom of East and West in some ways, although there is often a lot of distrust between people of different worldviews.

For a short while in 1975 I was involved with a macrobiotic community near Boston. This community was devoted to finding health and well-being through eating a balance of yin and yang foods. The yin side of things includes soft, dark, sweet, kind, and female. The yang side is hard, light, bitter, strict, and male. Most people's diet is much too yin with an emphasis on sugar, fat, cream, and alcohol. To bring balance one needs to eat yang foods, like short-grain brown rice, black radishes, green leaves, and seaweed. Somehow I was always afraid of showing up to a meeting with hot fudge sundae on my breath. People there told me that their founder became ill when he was old. After thinking through the possibilities for a long time he concluded that his system was too yang, which no one had ever heard of. So he basically went on a short diet of whiskey and ice cream, which seemed to help. We do need to work with the unexpected and surprising things in life rather than deny them.

Dualistic thinking has had a great influence on art, culture, philosophy, and politics. We can think of the dualistic basis of the Hegelian/Marxist dialectic with its thesis and antithesis, which engage dynamically through revolution and move toward the end, or synthesis, of Communism. These ideas were tried over several decades on a very large scale but finally proved to be unworkable at the end of the twentieth century. It seems to me that Communism is very religious in the sense that it requires faith in the vision of the prophet (Marx, Lenin, Mao, Stalin). Only through the priestly or prophetic vision of the prophet can we know what direction the dynamism of the revolution will take. The visions of the Communist prophets turned out not to fit reality.

There are many artistic examples of the Dualist worldview. One of the best known in film is the *Star Wars* series. *Stars Wars* involves a conflict between the forces of light, symbolized in the original movies by Luke Skywalker, and the forces of darkness, symbolized by Darth Vader. The solution and resolution of the tension between these two opposing elements is the Force, or a universal energy that is the source of everything and includes both a light and a dark side. There is, however, a problem with regarding the Force as totally unifying because light eventually triumphs over darkness in the *Star Wars* films. In other words, although the worldview of the films is Dualist, the conclusion is non-Dualist.

Although Dualism has been pervasive throughout our history, and has resulted in some practical applications involving health and living with balance, there are some difficulties with the second circle. One problem is that it doesn't really seem to be absolute. What is the opposite of a river? A desert is very different from a river, but is it the opposite? What is the opposite of time? Is it time running backwards? Is it eternity? There are many differences but not everything has a clear opposite. Somehow this absolute may not really be an absolute. It leaves some things out and so I begin to question Dualism as an adequate theory of everything.

Another difficulty is that, if the second circle is really absolute, then it has to include everything. It has to include both kindness and cruelty, and good and evil. If good and evil have to be brought into balance, however, then you can never have victory, because as soon as you have victory you have imbalance. The goal is harmony, not victory.

The Western tradition has long held that good and evil are not equal opposites. In the beginning there was good, and in the original context of good there came to be evil. In this view, evil cannot exist without goodness, but goodness can exist without evil. Most people hope that good overcomes evil, that kindness overcomes cruelty, that love overcomes hate. But the Dualist worldview doesn't allow for that.

A final problem with the second circle is that the harmony of opposites, if it's truly perfect and absolute, must be static. Nothing moves. If anything moves, the perfection is destroyed. When it's perfect it's absolutely still, and when it's absolutely still it's basically Monism—it's a unity. The second circle turns out to be the first circle rather than a totally distinct and separate worldview.

THE THIRD CIRCLE

Trinitarian

We can explore the third circle, Trinitarianism, using two approaches. The first approach involves looking around at everyday reality and asking: What could be the cause of this reality? The second approach involves using one of the basic sources of the Western worldview, the Bible, in order to see what it says about reality.

The first approach is called *natural* theology. It includes the kinds of things we learn through everyday observation and science. The second approach is called *revealed* theology. Revealed theology tells us things about reality that we could not figure out based on everyday observation and science.

Unfortunately, the two approaches, natural and revealed theology, are often seen as being in competition with each other. There are people on one extreme who insist that you can only understand reality through human observation and systematic reasoning, and people on the other extreme who are deeply suspicious of science and depend almost exclusively on the Bible. Understood rightly, I believe that the two approaches complement each other. Together they help enrich our view of reality, and for this reason I will make use of both of them in exploring the third circle.

The Problem of Opposites

According to the third circle, when we look around at the world we see both unity and diversity. In this way we are like the people of the first circle. But whereas the people of the first circle conclude that unity is good and diversity is not, and that unity is real and diversity is illusion, people of the third circle have a different view. They regard the original perfection, which is called God, as both perfectly unified and perfectly diversified.

We see a clear description of this reality in the Bible. God is perfectly unified as one God, and yet God is perfectly diversified in the three persons of the Father, Son, and Holy Spirit. There is unity and diversity in absolute reality. There is not one God who chooses to reveal Himself in three ways in order to create the appearance of diversity, and there are not three persons who choose to unite and cooperate in order to create the appearance of being unified. The original reality is 100% unified and 100% diversified. It's a 200% reality that cannot be comprehended by simple logic.

Here is a proverb I made up to capture the essence of this reality: *God alone is God, and God is not alone.* You cannot make this statement about any other God or original perfection. You can say *Buddha alone is Buddha,* but that is all. The rest is silence. You can say *Krishna alone is Krishna* and *Allah alone is Allah*, but the rest again is silence. If the God of the third circle wants to talk to somebody, He talks among Himself, because He is three persons. A God who wasn't diversified could not talk among Himself. He would have to create something else to talk with. He would require a creation in order to be personal, whereas the God of the third circle is intrinsically personal, independent of His creation. His creation does not complete Him but rather expresses Him.

If the original perfection is both unified and diversified, it means that when we experience unity in reality it shouldn't be a problem, and when we experience diversity in reality it shouldn't be a problem. In other words, unlike Monism, the third circle does not regard diversity as the cause of suffering, and does not see the solution to suffering as involving a detachment from diversity. Also, unlike Dualism, the third circle does not attempt to resolve suffering by balancing opposites. Instead, the third circle sees variation and contrast as a part of the original perfection, and therefore, as a normal part of reality itself.

Along with unity and diversity, there are other ways in which God's creation represents a 200% reality. For example, one of the images of reality described in the Bible is marriage. We see this reality at the start of the Bible in Genesis, when God brings Adam and Eve together, and we see it again at the end of the Bible in the marriage supper of the Lamb in the Book of Revelation. Now, is marriage more male or female? Most people would say it's equal. Does that mean it's 50–50? No, because if you take away the woman you don't have half of a marriage left. You have nothing. Marriage is 100% woman and 100% man. It's a new reality, a 200% reality that includes dimensionality and mystery.

That may seem odd, but the ancient Hebrews thought differently from the people of the European Enlightenment and most people today. We tend to think of reality in terms of flat pie charts where the whole can be divided up into separate parts that add up to 100%. We may divide this reality into unity and diversity, or we may divide it in terms of other 'difficult' opposites such as objectivity and subjectivity, or predestination and free will. But a flat pie chart will never give us a stable solution to these kinds of opposites. For example, in the case of predestination and free will, does God choose me or do I choose God? I could divide up the pie chart 50%–50%, but it doesn't seem like I should be equal to God, and so maybe I should make it 51% God and 49% me? Then again, maybe it should be 99% God and 1% me, or maybe 100% God and 0% me, or maybe 100% me and God is on a deistic holiday? None of this, of course, is satisfactory. The pie chart won't work. The third circle regards God as 100% sovereign and people as 100% responsible. God's sovereignty and the free will of people are both fully real. In this mysterious complementarity, Calvin and Arminius kiss each other.

Another way to think about the third circle is in terms of physical dimensions. Think of God's sovereignty as 100% of a two-dimensional plane and think of free will as 100% of another two-dimensional plane. If you intersect these two flat disks, as in the image below, you create a third dimension that includes both elements within a three-dimensional complementary reality.

Within this intersection there is no competition or contradiction of opposites. They fit together in a single and complementary reality. I think it's fitting that a God consisting of three persons should create a reality that has at least three dimensions.

Humpty Dumpty

If you find the idea of dimensions too dry and geometric, we can also express things in terms of *Humpty Dumpty*. Do you know Humpty Dumpty? He was an English egg. I don't know if he was a good egg or a bad egg, but he was certainly a profound egg. Humpty Dumpty represents everybody. The nursery rhyme tells us that Humpty Dumpty sat on a wall. There are two sides to a wall. There is the objective side and the subjective side. There is the predestination side and the free-will side, and many other opposites that make up reality. Humpty Dumpty fell off the wall, but which side did he fall on? The objective side or the subjective side? The predestination side or the free-will side? We do not know. It doesn't matter. He fell, and if you fall on either side of those divisions it's disastrous because you need both sides to have reality. When you fall on one side you are dead because you have only half of reality.

So, Humpty Dumpty fell—there he was, poor egg, shattered and splattered on the ground.

Remember how the poem goes?

> Humpty Dumpty sat on a wall
> Humpty Dumpty had a great fall
> All the King's horses and all the King's men
> Couldn't put Humpty together again.

Good night children! Sweet dreams! We laugh but it's awful, isn't it? Many nursery rhymes are grim probably because the lives of children can be so hard. These little songs are quite profound. According to the third circle, however, the *Humpty Dumpty* rhyme is missing a line. A fifth line belongs to the poem, a line that will transform it into a glorious and hopeful poem. The line is this:

> But the King could.

The King's horses and King's men couldn't do it, but the King could. The pastors and the missionaries and the evangelists and the scientists couldn't do it, but the King could. The King is the God of the third circle. He is the solution to the cause of suffering.

So how exactly does He do it?

Falling in Love on a Bridge

Before we can fully understand the solution to the cause of suffering, we need to go deeper into the third circle. Let's explore objectivity and subjectivity a little further, because they are such common ideas in everyday reality. People have argued for centuries over which one is more true. Throughout European history, scientists (especially those of the Enlightenment) have believed in objective truth, and artists have believed in subjective truth. Nowadays, modernists believe in objective truth, and postmodernists gravitate to a more subjective truth.

As I have already suggested, however, the objective and subjective cannot really be divided from each other. Consider a desk. When I look at my desk, I see four legs, and I see a certain size and shape. When you look at my desk, you will likely agree on the size and shape, and on the number of legs, unless you look from a different point of view and only see three or two legs. If we each took a ruler, and we each measured the different parts of the desk, our measurements (assuming we were alert and careful) would agree exactly. But each of us also sees the desk subjectively. When I see my desk, I see the desk of my high school chemistry teacher, and I see the teacher himself, Mr. Corbett, standing beside it. But you wouldn't see him. You couldn't. In the presence of my desk, my seeing four legs and Mr. Corbett is a part of reality. My perception and my memories are not objective, but they are true—not objectively true, but subjectively true. They are not false.

We often argue over which half of reality is true. I do not believe in objective truth, but I also don't believe in subjective truth. I believe all truth is both objective and subjective. Another way of saying this is that we have accurate truth, which is objective, and we have non-accurate truth, which is subjective. The two belong together in a complementary manner in reality. If you want to build a bridge, you have to approach it objectively by making accurate physical measurements at every step of the process. If you do so, then, in the end, you will have a true bridge. But you cannot fall in love accurately. The process is chaotic. But a relationship of love is not false. Nor is it objective. The objectivity of the bridge is the same for everybody, but the subjectivity of falling in love is unique and exclusive. A complete experience of truth might be falling in love on a bridge.

In a similar way, the Bible includes two kinds of truth. One is accurate truth, the other is non-accurate truth. When the Bible gives us historical facts they are accurate truth. You can test them and do research about them. The parables of Jesus, however, are not accurate. You cannot research the name of the prodigal son because he never existed as a fact. The parables are not accurately true but they are profoundly true as windows and doors of subjective perception into reality. People can come to the truth of the parables uniquely from any point of view or set of circumstances.

Another way of expressing a full concept of truth is to say: Fact plus meaning equals Truth. Fact is objective, and meaning is subjective. When I work with students on various topics they often ask me, 'What does that mean?' I make their eyes roll when I ask them, 'What does *meaning* mean?'

In the most basic sense, *meaning* means relationships. There is fact, and there is the relationship of that fact to other facts, and that relationship is meaning. A fact has no meaning in isolation. The color red has no meaning in itself. It only has meaning in its relationship with blue or green or yellow. In the same way, you have no meaning in yourself but only in your relationship with your environment and other people.

Adam, according to the biblical account of creation, had no meaning in himself. When God made Adam, He said: *It is not good for man to be alone.* Adam was only a fact, only objective, because his was the only point of view within the creation. True subjectivity requires more than one viewpoint. God made Eve, and then it was good. There was subjectivity in the creation—just as there is in the Creator—as a result of relationship.

We see the same expression of meaning in God. In the original perfection of the third circle you have three persons, and the persons have no meaning in themselves.

The meaning of Jesus is not in Jesus. The meaning of Jesus is in His relationship with the Father and the Holy Spirit. The same is true of the other two—their meaning is in their relationship with each of the others. They also see each other from a different point of view. The Son, for instance, sees the Father from a different point of view than the Holy Spirit does. What they see is slightly different from each other, but they each see perfectly. These differences are a great liberation. It means we don't have to be clones of each other. We don't have to have the same taste. There can be true variety of point of view and reaction. Difference of perspective is a part of absolute reality, of the original perfection.

When we find out that the original perfection is like this—a true God who is both objective and subjective—then we shouldn't be surprised to experience objectivity and subjectivity in our reality. Nor should we think that one of them is the cause of suffering. But we often do. An artistic person may think that objective truth has no freedom and is the cause of suffering. A scientist may argue that subjectivity has no stable or reliable form and is the cause of suffering. The Bible describes an absolute truth that is objectively one God and subjectively three persons. Objectivity and subjectivity belong to each other in reality. Their relationship is not competitive but complementary.

Defying Gravity

Freedom and form is another pair of opposites that we see in the world. A good illustration is gravity. Gravity is one of the basic forms, or structures, of reality, but it gives us a certain freedom. If gravity were not here and I began to walk, I would float and spin and soon I would be dead. Form, or structure, is necessary. Let me give you an equation to express this idea:

$$total\ freedom = death$$

There is nothing postmodern about this equation. Postmodernism, as usually understood and practiced in Western culture, regards freedom as the highest value, and sees the purpose of freedom as fun and play. But freedom cannot really be valuable or life-giving unless it is accompanied by form. If you want to be totally free to fly, you can go to the top of a building and jump. You can say, 'I am free!' But you won't be free, you will be dead, because you have not respected form. But if you study the various forms of reality—the laws and properties that give reality structure and shape, such as gravity, aerodynamics, thermodynamics, metallurgy, jet propulsion, stress, torque, and so on—then you will be able to build an airplane and fly across the ocean. That's a great freedom, but the freedom is completely connected to form. Freedom and form are not independent of each other in reality. Again, their relationship is complementary rather than competitive.

What about God? The three persons of God give Him particular forms. The persons do not have the same form as each other. The form of the Father is to command and to send. The form of the Son is to obey and to go. Their forms are opposite in some ways, but they are both God. The form of the Holy Spirit is to hover over creation, to blow as a wind, and to indwell, teach and empower human beings. When each of these persons is faithful to His form, He is also free to be God. But if any of them were not faithful to His form then the creation would be destroyed, because the creation is dependent on the form of the Creator. If the Creator is unfaithful to His own character, the foundation is no longer there. The freedom and the form of God are both eternal. They must both be constant by His constant choosing.

For this reason, God is not automatic in being the way He is. He chooses to be faithful to His forms, and it costs something. The clearest way to see this cost is in the Garden of Gethsemane. Jesus, in staying faithful to the form of His promise, has come into creation in order to die for it and therefore to save it. The moment is coming to do that, and He realizes He doesn't want to. He prays to the Father, saying, *Please, if it can be any other way, let it be.* As He prays, the blood comes out of His skin and runs down onto the ground. He is experiencing intense stress. What does this mean?

It means He is struggling. He is not automatic. He is God, working, serving, giving, praying, in order to be Himself, for Himself and for us. There is no other God like that.

If form and freedom are a part of the original perfection, then they are not the cause of suffering. In other words, although we may suffer in the context of varying degrees of freedom in life, or varying degrees of form, we will not find salvation by simply getting rid of all forms or structures or by focusing only on freedom and possibilities. We need both form and freedom in our lives, because they are a part of the original perfection.

Change, Time, and Eternity

Dynamism is another aspect of the third circle. Dynamism means that things are not static. They change in relationship to each other. Reality involves before and during and after. In the first letter of Peter, we are told that before the world was made, the Son was chosen by the Father to come into the world and save it. In other words—before there was space and time—there was before the choosing, during the choosing, and after the choosing.

Dynamism occurs in two matrixes of sequence. I mean *matrix* in the same sense as in the movie *The Matrix*—an environment or context in which things happen. Water is the matrix of tea, meaning that tea happens in water. Cyberspace is the matrix of e-mail, meaning that e-mail happens in cyberspace. The matrix of sequence *in space* is time, meaning that everything that happens happens in time. The matrix of sequence *outside of space* is eternity. Many people think that eternity is infinite time, but that isn't how the Bible describes it. Eternity is a separate matrix of sequence in that every point of time is present to every point of eternity. That is why prophecy is possible. God lives in eternity, and from every point of the dynamic matrix of eternity, all of time is present.

This vision of absolute reality is different from what we see in Monism and Dualism. Monism regards dynamism as illusory and unreal. Dualism regards the original perfection as the harmony of opposites, which, if absolute and perfect, must be static and without any change. In the Zen view, you would say *I enter the water and I make no ripples, because everything is always the same.* There is no motion.

The third circle sees dynamism as a real and non-illusory part of absolute reality. God is dynamic and His creation is dynamic. For this reason, dynamism cannot be regarded as the cause of suffering.

Me and We

Another major element of the third circle, and one that Christians like to emphasize, is that God is a *personal* God. I couldn't agree more with this statement. But God is not a personal God because I personally believe in Him. He is not a personal God because I have a personal relationship with Him. God was a personal God before I was born. That He is personal is completely independent of creation, and stems from there being three persons in relationship with each other.

In this respect, God's nature tells us something about how we need to understand personality. Most psychological models present personality as a description of the individual. The same model has been adopted by the modern church, which sometimes defines people in terms of body, soul, and spirit. The problem with this idea is that it's all about the individual, whereas the biblical description of the person places primary emphasis on relationship. You see this reality in God's own nature, as separate persons in relationship, and you see it in the beginning of creation, when God created people in His own image. When Adam was still alone—when he was self-aware, and aware of his environment and of naming the animals—he was still not personal because he didn't have any relationships within the creation. He could relate to God outside of the creation but within the creation the image of God was not complete until it was *we* or *us* rather than *I* or *me*. The image of God is *we* based on relationships. Also, in a right relationship of man and woman as God originally designed it, there is a third person—a child. God is three persons and His image comes in sets of three persons.

The emphasis on relationship does not mean that the individual does not matter, or that individual identity is somehow lost. Individuality is completely retained but understood first and foremost in the context of relationship. Personality is self-aware consciousness in relationship with other self-aware consciousness. It can be difficult to accept this view of the person. It seems to put things in the wrong order. Many of us would prefer to define ourselves first by our identity and personal characteristics and second by our relationships. In the opening lines of the Gospel of John, we are told:

In the beginning was the Word, and the Word was…
How does the verse end?

People who don't know the verse expect it to say:
…and the Word was God.

But it doesn't say that. It says:
…and the Word was with God, and the Word was God.

Relationship comes first, then identity.
Relationship precedes identity.

You Gotta Serve Somebody

If relationship is a part of absolute reality, then it cannot be the cause of suffering. Relationship also brings with it a number of other elements. One of them is hierarchy. Hierarchy refers to relationships of authority. It means that some individuals have authority under certain circumstances—have the power and responsibility to describe reality—while other people are under authority. In our culture hierarchy feels wrong. It's politically incorrect. From a biblical perspective, however, hierarchy is a part of God's nature, and so it must be a part of reality itself.

An example of hierarchy is the relationship between parents and children. Parents have authority over small children. They have authority to describe bedtime and diet, and to describe play in the garden rather than in the street. Small children need this authority to describe reality for them in order to survive. They cannot adequately describe reality for themselves. Now, who is more human in this relationship, the parents or the children? You will say, of course, that they are equally human. But in other relationships you might hesitate. If you have a boss and an employee, who is more human? If you have beautiful, successful people on the one hand, and ugly failures on the other, who is more human? If you have rich people and poor people, who is more human? We get confused by this. We think that in hierarchical relationships, some people are more real or more valuable than others. This idea, however, belongs to the culture of a fallen world. It belongs to the church of a fallen world. It isn't the idea God wants us to have.

Hierarchy does not imply inequality of value or significance. In God, the Father commands and the Son obeys, and they are equally God. The Son is not an apprentice god waiting to get His certificate. He is not a junior god waiting to graduate. He is fully and eternally God, and He obeys. This view of God doesn't fit with our current culture because we think we are more human and alive when we command and less human when we obey. That can't be true if we're made in the image of God. To obey is equally divine as to command, and so to obey is equally human as to command. Hierarchy and authority are grossly misused, unfortunately, and this misuse causes great suffering. If hierarchy is a part of God, however, then it cannot in itself be the cause of suffering. Bob Dylan gets it right when he says *you gotta serve somebody*.

The Bible describes five basic relationships of authority. These are husbands and wives, parents and children, masters and slaves (or employers and employees in contemporary terms), the state and citizens, and elders and members of churches. That covers most of the major hierarchies of life. God, according to the Bible, has given us those relationships, and those relationships are good.

But they also malfunction. We experience suffering in all of those relationships. They don't work right. Sometimes, when we see that a relationship doesn't work right, we think that the solution is to eliminate the relationship. In the Western world, we find that marriage is problematic. Many people believe they can solve the problem by not having marriage. But I don't think that's going to be a solution, because that relationship is given by God.

It doesn't help to pretend that marriage is perfect. Marriage takes work in order to create a relationship of love and support. We must also be careful not to assume that the husband, who has authority, is more valuable and real than the wife. We must not assume that having authority justifies the abuse of power. The Bible doesn't give us that picture. C. S. Lewis wrote a book called *The Four Loves*, and one of the things he tells us is that the husband and father in a family should wear a crown, but it should be a crown of thorns. I think that's a good picture. He wears a crown and he is bleeding. He suffers. He carries the weight. That's an interesting balance, isn't it? If we look in the Bible itself, we hear Paul teaching us that the husband is to be like Christ to the wife, which means he should die to make her beautiful. That's an extreme picture. That's not politically correct. That does not fit in our world. It sounds ridiculous. But it's what the Bible gives us. There is a conflict between what the Bible gives us and the world we live in, and we need to think about and struggle with the conflict to find the right way.

Look, Daddy, Look!

Another aspect of relationship, and of the third circle in general, is needs. We all experience needs. We need to eat and drink and be warm and to live under a roof, but more deeply than that we need to be seen. You see it with small children. All day children will cry, 'Look, Daddy, look!' If it's a choice between eating lunch or Daddy-looking, getting Daddy's attention always wins because it's a more basic need. To be seen by Daddy or Mommy or other people that matter is more important than eating. And if Daddy and Mommy don't look because they're at work all the time or divorced or drunk or in jail or dead, or always on a missionary trip, then the need is not met and the child is horribly distorted and will suffer. That describes all of us.

We also need to be heard. Even before a child masters language, they coo and babble, making noises to be heard. It's painful for children when they are not heard. As adults we still need people to hear us when we speak, even if they disagree. It's deeply frustrating not to be heard. It diminishes our humanness.

We also need to make a difference. We need to have an effect on the world. If a child takes some blocks and piles them on top of each other, they're not the same as before.

They're different. *I did that* the child can say—and then the child knocks it down. Different again. Sometimes the child's need is not convenient, like when he or she smears lipstick on the wall, but you can still see the need to make a difference. It goes on through our entire lives. If we bake bread we need people to eat it. If we build a house people should live in it. Where I have been and lived and worked should not be the same as if I had not been there. This is how God made us to be.

Related to all of these needs is the need to be wanted. We need people to say 'Come, be with me, be with us, you are wanted.'

Why do we have these needs? Is it the result of sin? Do they come from the devil? Are these needs a temptation? You might say we have these needs because we are only human, but who defines what it means to be a human? According to the third circle, human beings are made in God's image. Their needs come from God because God has these needs. Maybe you have never thought about God having needs? It's not that God needs anything from *us*. Rather, He has needs among Himself, and exactly the same needs we have—to be seen, to be heard, to make a difference, and to be wanted. But God does not suffer from these needs. Having these needs is pure joy for God, because needs are the basis for trust and love. A need that can only be fulfilled by another person requires that you trust that person to fulfill it. If there were no needs, there would be no real trust or love.

Before there was any creation, when there was only God, there was already trust and love in reality because there was already a fulfillment of the need to be seen and be heard and make a difference and be wanted. Each of the three persons of God fills the needs of the other persons, and does so by emptying Himself for the others. Jesus empties Himself for the Father and the Holy Spirit. For this reason, the center of reality for Jesus is not in Jesus, it's in the Father and Holy Spirit. Each of the persons of God is similarly other-centered rather than centered in Himself. Such is the Bible's depiction of absolute reality: a totally other-centered God. This other-centeredness is the source of God's energy, for as each of the persons of God empties Himself once, He is filled twice by the others. This energy increases exponentially. It became so great that God could say *Let there be light!* and a universe was born. The Bible gives a name to this energy when it says *God is love*. It is an other-centered emptying and filling, a perpetual building up of energy. It is the energy of life. It is the foundation of all reality.

Notice that the Bible doesn't only say *God is loving* or *He loves*, although these are true. It's far more radical— God *is* love. Notice also that it says *God is just* but it doesn't say 'God is justice' because He's also merciful. And it doesn't say 'God is mercy' because He's also just. But when it says *God is love* it doesn't contrast that with anything. Love is the total reality of what God is.

Just as God is fully other-centered, we too were meant to be this way. When Adam was alone within the creation, God saw that it was not good, and so He made Eve. Now the identity of Adam could be fully outside of himself in relationship. The center of Adam was not in Adam; it was in Eve and it was in God. The center of Eve was not in Eve; it was in God and in Adam. The creation reflected the Creator. It's for this reason that we, like God, continue to have needs, and it's for this reason that we yearn for these needs to be fulfilled within relationships of love and trust with each other and with God.

If needs are a part of the original perfection, then they cannot be the cause of suffering. We may indeed suffer when our needs are not met, but the needs themselves are not the fundamental reason why things are not right in the world.

Up to now, along with needs, we have considered unity and diversity, objectivity and subjectivity, predestination and free will, form and freedom, dynamism, personality and relationships, and hierarchy—and *none of them*, according to the third circle, is the real cause of suffering in our world.

So what is? And what is the solution?

A Black Hole in the Heart

In the book of Genesis, we're told that God put the Tree of the Knowledge of Good and Evil in the Garden with Adam and Eve. And God said: *Do not eat the fruit of this tree. You must not know good and evil for yourselves. You must trust Me to tell you.*

You might wonder why God gave them the option of eating the fruit. Why not prevent them from doing it? Why not put a barbed wire fence around the tree? The reason, as I mentioned earlier, is that God is not automatic, and so His creation cannot be automatic either. Just as God is free to choose, and He chooses always to be faithful to Himself, we as the image of God are given the same choice—the choice to be trusting and dependent upon Him. So the possibility exists that we can choose wrongly.

I ought to point out that if God is non-automatic, then the possibility also exists that *He* can choose wrongly. There is nobody behind God forcing Him to fulfill His promises. God Himself must choose to do so. As I suggested earlier, you see the possibility for choosing wrongly in the Garden of Gethsemane. If there was no possibility that Jesus would fail to fulfill His promise, then He would not have sweat blood. He would not have prayed, *Please, if it can be any other way, let it be.* You see the same possibility a few years earlier in Jesus' life, when He is tempted by the devil while in the desert. The temptation would have been completely meaningless if there was no possibility for Jesus to have fallen for it. Thankfully, that God has never broken His promises and even died in order to keep them is clear assurance that He will always be faithful.

So, the origin of the possibility of evil is in God, but there is no evil in God. The creatures that God made in His image also have this possibility, and their choices have often resulted in tragedy. The best known example is the devil. He was, at one time, the most beautiful of all angels but chose to turn away from God. Did you ever notice that the devil is just one person, whereas God is three? The devil is *one* because he is exclusively self-centered. It is his absolute self-centeredness that makes him absolutely evil.

According to Genesis, the devil came to Eve in the Garden and said, *Did God say you couldn't eat anything?* Eve replied, *Oh no, we can eat anything we want, we just can't eat of that tree.* And the devil said, *If you eat of that tree, you will become like God, because God knows good and evil and you will also know good and evil. You won't have to bother God about telling you about good and evil, you'll know for yourself. You can be independent. You can be a liberated woman.* That was appealing to Eve. She was intelligent, she had an adventurous spirit. She took another look at the tree and saw that the fruit was very attractive, and she knew that she really would have the knowledge of good and evil if she ate it, and would be self-sufficient. She wouldn't need God to tell her.

After eating it, Eve gave some to Adam, and then he ate it. At that moment they both died. I don't mean they had heart attacks and fell over. I mean their relationship and their identity died. They knew that they were naked. They knew they were a threat to each other. There was no longer trust. They didn't trust God and they couldn't trust each other. When their relationship died, they were dead. Their true identity had not been in themselves but in their relationship.

Adam and Eve realized there was a problem, and sometimes I think they could have held hands and gone to God and said, 'Father, we have a problem, can you help us?' But they didn't do that because they had become insane. Their thinking was now fundamentally distorted and unhealthy. Instead of going to the Creator for a solution, they reached into creation. They found fig leaves and sewed them together to hide their sexuality, probably because that was what they now found most disturbing and threatening. In reaching into the creation for a solution, we also see the birth of *naturalism*, a belief that we should turn to the physical world in order to solve our problems.

God came into the Garden and called for Adam. Why did He want to talk to Adam if Eve was the one who took the first bite? Here you see the function of hierarchy. Adam was with Eve when she did it, and he was responsible for her. For this reason, God wants to know from Adam what has happened. That's not politically correct, but that's the way God does it.

In confronting Adam, God asks a wonderful question: *Where are you?* Remember that God knows everything. The question is not for God to get information. The question is for Adam, so that he can ask himself where he is. Adam gives a good answer when he replies, *I'm in fear, and nakedness, and hiding.* That was all true. That was his situation.

Then God asks a second question: *Who told you that you were naked?* In other words 'What are your sources and why have you believed them?' He also asks: *Have you eaten of the fruit that I told you not to eat? Did you bring this fear and nakedness and hiding on yourself?* Adam's answer, in this case, could not be worse. He says, *The woman, who you gave to me, offered me the fruit. It's your fault and her fault.* In other words 'I am a victim.' It was here that victimization and denial began. 'I'm not responsible, I'm a victim. I don't need to be forgiven, I'm entitled. I don't need to confess and repent.' This attitude has remained popular in the human race.

God made coats from the skins of animals and clothed them. He killed the innocent and He covered Adam and Eve with the blood of the innocent. It was a visual and applied prophecy of the Crucifixion. Here, and in many other episodes described in the Bible, you can also see how the God of the third circle is not a passive and silent God. He is not a New Age elephant. He is active and communicative. From the beginning, He is deeply engaged with His creation and working faithfully toward its salvation.

Salvation is necessary because ever since the unfaithfulness of Adam and Eve we have been living in a condition of self-centeredness. The human condition has imploded like a supernova—like a huge star that has exploded outward and then reversed direction and collapsed into a black hole, whose gravity is so strong that not even light can escape from it. Everything gets sucked into it. Self-centeredness is what it means to be dead. It's what it means to be a sinner. It's a disastrous situation, and, according to the third circle, it's the cause of suffering in the world.

The Solution

So how do we get out of this mess? The solution is that the Creator Himself enters into the creation and becomes one of us, a human being, made of flesh and blood. Hence the birth of Jesus: *Merry Christmas!* Then, being in the creation and being the Creator, in time and in eternity, natural and supernatural, human and God, immanent and transcendent, He does one thing: He empties Himself. Literally. He sacrifices His life, allowing His body to be nailed to a wooden cross, so that His blood can be drained for others. Jesus gave Himself, emptied Himself, not for Himself but for others. It was, and remains, the ultimate, most astonishing other-centered act in all of history.

The crucifixion of Jesus wasn't just an idea. It wasn't a symbolic gesture. It was an actual, physical emptying for others. Jesus saved us with His blood. We are broken, and God came into the creation and emptied Himself. The power of that emptying, which is dying to self, kills death. Death was killed on the cross. The death that Jesus died was not caused by sin. It was not caused by self-centeredness. The death that Jesus died was caused by perfect love, and so the death was perfect and swallowed up all of death in victory.

This behavior is typical God-behavior. It's the basic nature of God. God is love, and love, according to the first letter of John, is an atoning sacrifice. Atonement means *making it possible to be together*. The meaning is easily remembered if we break the word down into three parts: at–one–ment. Our sin, or self-centeredness, separates us from God, each other and the rest of creation, and Jesus came to make atonement so that we could be together. Jesus shows us what it means to be in the image of God.

Notice that Jesus didn't die on earth and He didn't die in heaven. He was hanging on a cross, suspended in the middle: He bridges heaven and earth. The Roman emperor in those days was called *pontifex maximus*, the Great Bridge Builder, but the title is more fitting for the crucified Christ who connects the Creator and the creation, eternity and time, the immanent and the transcendent, bringing all things together by the power of His word, by the power of His blood, making a new reality. Reality has been divided by sin, and His body is the bridge that crosses the divide. This is Jesus Christ. This is the God-man.

The result of Jesus' death was three days in the tomb, earthquake, darkness, and then resurrection. Resurrection was not resuscitation of a dead body into life. The resurrected body of Christ was raised not like Lazarus who was raised to die again, but to eternal life, into a glorified existence.

The Bible tells us that people who receive the power of

Jesus' blood will also become new people. God is a choice-making God, and we as His image are a choice-making people, and so we must choose to receive the power to be remade. It isn't a change of mind. It isn't joining a club. It's a radical turn of being. When we choose to receive the power of the blood of Jesus we are remade. We have been dead self-centered creatures who become living other-centered creatures. The expression the Bible uses to describe this change is *born again*. When we are born as babies, we cannot become unborn, and we eventually die. When we are born again by the blood of Christ, we cannot become unborn, and we do not die. We become new creatures that belong in a new heaven and new earth. We are remade in the power of the Crucifixion. We are no longer self-centered, imploding, dead individuals, but we are re-created as other-centered living people.

Once we have been born again, the rest of our lives is a process of adjusting to becoming other-centered. We grow in love. Our life gets bigger and richer. That is the picture the Bible gives us. It isn't the picture that we see very much in our world. We don't see it much in ourselves; we don't see it much in the church, but it's the picture of God's deepest desire for us. It's a real power that is available to us in Jesus, at this very moment—to become new creatures, turned inside out, reborn, emptying ourselves, losing our lives in order to find them.

That is the Christian solution to suffering.

To Put it Simply

We have explored three circles, or three absolute worldviews, each of which provides a unique hope to the problem of suffering. In the first circle, the original perfection is a total perfect unity and we suffer because we have the illusion of diversity. Salvation is waking up and realizing that unity again. In the second circle, the original perfection is the perfect harmony of equal opposites. We suffer because disharmony or imbalance has come into reality. Salvation is restoring that harmony and balance through various methods and therapies. In the third circle, the original perfection is a unity of three persons who are other-centered in a relational reality of love. We suffer because we have turned things around and have become self-centered dead people. Salvation is God coming into creation and giving Himself in order that people can receive the power to be re-created as other-centered living people.

What do you think? Where are you?

45 QUESTIONS

Asking honest questions is a sign of life. During the many years I have lectured and spoken with people about the three circles, hundreds of questions have been raised. Such questions are invaluable as they connect people more directly and practically with my teaching and keep us away from mechanical on–off, black–white responses. We grow and learn by asking.

My hope is that the following questions, translated from various languages, may stimulate your thoughts and provoke further topics for discussion among you.

o o o

Do you truly believe it's possible to simplify so vast and complex a subject as the cosmos into one of your theoretical circles?

No, it's not. The three circles are grossly reductionistic symbol sets. I hope they will be useful, but they are not adequate. Objective truth in the form of a symbol is not sufficient to express the Truth. Truth is also subjective, which means that explanations involving symbols must be combined with your personal subjective experience to produce reality. You cannot merely think about Jesus and be a Christian any more than you can think about matrimony and have a marriage. The reality of being married is much larger than any kind of symbol. Still, symbols can be helpful.

What is the Monist's view of spiritual evolution?

In most cases people in the first circle see the human being as a high level of consciousness, evolved from a life force that manifests itself in increasingly complex ways and increasingly self-aware ways. Animals, such as flies or worms or rats, would not have individual consciousness. The human being has individual consciousness and makes choices as an individual. The human is also reincarnated in the same consciousness, albeit without an awareness of the past, whereas the consciousness of the rat or fly would dissolve into unconsciousness when it dies. Although other life-forms suffer, they don't have the possibility to realize unity and stop suffering until they evolve and focus in human individual consciousness. To be a human being in terms of the whole of reality is considered very precious. The human being has the possibility of enlightenment. The belief that humans live and die thousands of times might also make people of the first circle more patient. If you don't manage something in this life, don't panic, because there is another life. This view can make you more relaxed and reduce stress, which in many ways can be healthy. Still, we need to consider things within the whole context of what is real and to ask, 'Do we pay too big a price for the therapy that we experience?'

How do people of monistic religions see marriage?

In the first circle, marriage is something that people do as a helpful exercise in the early stages of development, because marriage is a form of uniting and becoming one. But when you are very advanced in your incarnations, you go and live in a monastery. There are very religious people in India who get married and raise children and have a business, but when their children leave home they sometimes sell the business and separate, and one goes to a monastery and the other goes to a nunnery. They release each other for advancement, because they realize that they have become a handicap to each other. They have experienced a union in the marriage, but it's also an attachment. They have to separate in order to increase in Buddha-nature or Krishna consciousness.

How do people of monistic religions explain increases or changes in the human population?

The appearance of more human beings on the earth reflects the movement of more groups of life-forms into human individual consciousness. Those individual consciousnesses are manifest in the birth of babies. A new baby may be someone who is born for the thousandth time or for the first time. The baby could be much older than the parents in terms of evolutionary progression. That might be an explanation for the genius of Mozart; he may have been an older person with lots of experience behind him. The population of humans can get larger or smaller according to the wisdom of the Lords of Karma. Human beings function under the decisions of the Lords of Karma, which deals with so many variables that we cannot comprehend them.

You suggested that there is no genuine right and wrong in Monism. Doesn't the idea of karma, however, implicitly recognize the concepts of right and wrong, and therefore a general moral structure?

Karma operates within the illusion of maya, of diversity, of particularity and relationships. In that illusion there are positive and negative situations, energies, and vibrations that are established and created and which need to be brought into harmony in order for Buddha-nature or Krishna consciousness to be realized. Karma is an extremely rich and complicated process. The long-range goal is to become liberated in Buddha-nature or Krishna consciousness. The working out of karma, however, can occur in a variety of ways. Consider the example of murder. If I murder somebody in this lifetime, then in my next lifetime I might be murdered, or I might save lives. Either possibility could produce a balance in my karma, even though the two possibilities are very different. One is passive and results in death, the other is active and results in life. Karma is not a retributive judicial system. It has that element in it, but there are other major elements intertwined with it, so you can't understand karma purely in moral terms. It's larger and broader and richer than that.

You mentioned that in the monistic worldview relationships are evil, and love is also evil, because love is a relationship. If this is the case, then why does Buddhism emphasize compassion so strongly?

Your question equates compassion with love, which is a mistake. Love involves relationship, but compassion is a realization of unity and identity. When I have compassion for someone, I support their movement toward the realization of Buddha-nature or Krishna consciousness in the context of many, many reincarnated lifetimes. Let me give you an example. If a person is born into a life of suffering, it's possible they may be working out their karma based on the wisdom of the Lords of Karma about what is most profitable for that person. For this reason, if I see that person suffering, I should avoid helping him because I understand that he might have to suffer all over again if I interfere in his process. This reasoning is the basis for the Buddhist doctrine of non-interference. It may seem cruel not to help a suffering person, but in the context of reincarnation it might be the most compassionate thing to do, because by not interfering with the person's suffering you are allowing that person to bring their karma into balance. The Christian idea of love is very different, because the context in which it occurs is very different. There is only one lifetime in which all significance of our being and choice-making is concentrated. There is also a fundamental belief in the eternal reality of relationships. The love of Christ is a love of relationships, of seeing face-to-face, of encouraging each other to be ourselves as God made us to be. Poverty and suffering are seen as distortions of God's intention for human life and are things to be worked against. Christians have a mandate to relieve the suffering of others and to respect everybody's individual life. So compassion and love are not synonymous, although we hear them used that way in the culture at large. The Bible has the word compassion, but it's very closely connected to love.

Buddhism recognizes that depression and other forms of emotional suffering are connected to narcissism, egotism, and an obsession with the self, and it provides methods to treat this suffering. In what ways does Christianity add to our understanding of emotional suffering and healing?

The idea that depression and emotional suffering are a result of narcissism and egotism is, in many cases, quite accurate. The same basic idea can be found in the Bible. The Buddhist and Christian perspectives differ, however, with respect to the context of the suffering and the cure. For Buddhists, the choice is between self and SELF, between individual egocentric self and universal Buddha-nature SELF. The Christian choice is between self-centered and other-centered. As a result, the Buddhist solution to suffering has the goal of dissolving the self into the absolute SELF. The Christian solution has the goal of reorienting the self in the direction of *others*—toward other people and toward God. The individual self is preserved, not dissolved, and heals and develops through a relationship of love with the rest of reality. That is the basic meaning of salvation through Jesus Christ. Christianity values the need to heal depression, and it values healing practices in general (whether Buddhist or otherwise), but it would not sacrifice the unique reality of the person, of God, or the reality of love, in exchange for healing or freedom from suffering.

New Age people emphasize the power of belief. What do you think of that?

The idea, if I understand it, is that we create reality through our thinking. If we think negatively we create a more negative reality, and if we think positively we produce a more positive reality. Positive thinking in biblical terms always occurs in the context of Jesus. It's not really about *us* creating reality but trusting that God will create *for* us the reality that we need in order to carry out His purpose for our lives. What He creates might please us, or it might be at odds with what we want. Either way, we should be grateful and trusting and work with what God gives us.

If children color mandalas in school, will they be drawn to Hinduism?

Maybe, but they will be no more drawn to Hinduism by coloring mandalas than to Jesus by coloring crosses.

Is meditation dangerous for Christians?

It would be different for different people. For some people, it could be therapeutic. For some psychological conditions it could be very dangerous. It's also very dangerous if we think that meditating will forgive our sins, or that it will give us our true identity, or if we meditate instead of praying.

Is there a Christian practice of meditation?

The phrase 'Christian practice of meditation' is associated with a whole history and practice of ideas that is too large to address here. Allow me to narrow the question to a more specific consideration of the *biblical* practice of meditation. While Eastern meditation seeks to stop the mind or hold it still, biblical meditation starts with some content about God, holds it over the mind as over a web or net, and allows the Holy Spirit to touch the mind with it. Then the person thinks and prays about the connection they have experienced. Biblical meditation is not directional and does not have an agenda. It's more passive and receptive than thinking, but it is connected to thinking.

Atheism is a major worldview today. Where does it fit among your three circles?

Atheism is the belief that there is no God and that all things emerge by chance from the material substance of the universe. Many atheists believe that the universe began with a singularity, or a unity of all energy in a single point that exploded outward in an event called the *big bang*. After the big bang, diversity is believed to have entered the universe through the emergence of various physical laws and physical phenomena including stars, planets, and eventually the earth with its various characteristics, including biological life as we know it. None of these physical facts, however, can have absolute meaning in atheism. Atheists can experience a *feeling* of meaning, in the sense of feeling as if their life is meaningful, or as if their relationships are meaningful, or as if sunsets and mountain ranges are meaningful, but if there is no actual absolute meaning in the universe—if the universe is an impersonal and accidental thing—then anything that occurs within the universe cannot be absolutely meaningful either, no matter how much we may feel or believe it to be. In an atheistic universe, meaning is essentially an illusion. Although atheists may not regard themselves as Monists, you can see the similarity in their viewpoints: the universe begins in a state of unity, and then gives rise to a diversity that is actually an illusion. People of the third circle, on the other hand, assume that the universe and everything in it is absolutely meaningful because it was created by a God who is intrinsically meaningful. Life, as a result, is not fundamentally an illusion. It seems to me to take a great deal more faith to be an atheist than to be a Christian, because you have to maintain the idea that a blind, meaningless, purposeless, amoral, uncaring, directionless reality has produced human beings who are the opposite of all these characteristics. A simpler assumption is that the characteristics of humanness are an expression of something inherent within the universe itself, and something that pre-exists the universe. To paraphrase the Bible: *in the beginning there was Information.*

I think the attraction of atheism for many people is that it relieves them of the burden of having to think deeply about *why* they exist. It also relieves them of any idea of guilt or sin. If there is no absolute meaning, there can be no real justification for feelings of guilt or a belief in right and wrong. Again, the lack of any absolute meaning in categories like right and wrong makes atheism quite similar to Monism. Some atheists also believe that after expanding for a period of time, the universe will collapse again into singularity, or total unity, which is not unlike the Monist's view. Other atheists, however, believe the universe will expand endlessly. Given the many similarities between Monism and atheism, I would say that atheism can be regarded as part of the first circle or a variation of the first circle.

Christians sometimes adopt a defensive posture to the good they see in non-Christians. An example would be a statement like: Well, it was nice of those atheists to contribute to a good cause, but—and the but may be followed by—they don't have Jesus, or they are going to hell in the end, or some other statement that has the effect of discounting the goodness of another human being. Have you witnessed this attitude toward non-Christian acts of goodness, and what thoughts do you have about it?

I have seen that attitude, but less recently than in previous years I'm glad to say. I think it's out of place in the kingdom of God not to recognize goodness when we see it, and not to believe that all human beings have eternity in their hearts. In a fundamental sense, it's not possible to please God without faith, but I think it's possible to express His image in a variety of ways, in some cases more accurately by the non-Christian than by the Christian. But those expressions of goodness, if they're not contextualized and completed by Jesus Christ, are not integrated. They are not held together. They are bits and snatches and incomplete. The goodness of the Christian, even if in some cases less than that of the non-Christian, is completed in Christ. In the idea of the writer of Hebrews, *all things are held together in Christ by the word of His power.* Either way, there is no room for sneering about another person's act of goodness. There is room for admiration and praise and self-rebuke.

Have you benefited from your contact with atheists?

Yes. I think I've learned something about what it means to be human and made in the image of God from atheists—in particular from those who practice patience and discipline in ways that I don't, and from those who practice creativity, courage, and the embrace of life in ways better than I have. So I have learned from some atheists about what it means to be a human being. I don't learn from them what it means to have my sins forgiven or to be completed in Christ, but I have learned lots of other things.

Into which of the three circles do animistic and shamanistic worldviews fit? Where would Judaism and Islam fit?

Remember that the circles are a reductionistic and approximated system. They address the fundamental aspects of different worldviews rather than surface details. Bearing this in mind, I suggest that animism and shamanism would fit into the first or second circle, or some combination of the two, depending on individual understanding or practices. Judaism as we find it in the Old Testament, or Torah, would fit the third circle. In the creation account, God speaks among Himself, and later He appeared to Abraham as three men. You have the whole Trinity in the Old Testament. In the understanding and practice and thought of Jews, however, you will see some leaning toward the first circle. In the Koran, you have fundamentally the first circle. Allah is one. There is no other. He has no son. There is a very strong unity and absoluteness in Allah. He is not intrinsically relational. If Allah wants to talk to somebody and function as a personal god, then he has to create somebody to talk to.

Some people might wonder why bother with worldviews? Why not just live life as best you can? What are your thoughts about that?

You can to a large extent try to live like that, without any particular direction or context. You couldn't hold any strong ideas, or have any committed purpose, because you wouldn't believe that anything was right or wrong, fitting or unfitting, and probably you would slip into the idea that 'what is right is what feels good, and what is wrong is what feels bad, and I am the judge. I am God.' At the same time, living life 'as best you can' implies a worldview of some kind, even if it's not clearly defined. That's a key issue. We all need a worldview to have a frame and foundation for any meaning and purpose in life, and to provide a justification for our actions. To put it another way, choosing to live as best you can requires some way to measure *best,* and the context of measuring *best* is a worldview. We can bother with the worldview or not, acknowledge it or not, but it's always there.

Do you think the simpler life is happier and more joyful?

Not necessarily. Riches and money and property and knowledge can add burdens to our lives, and give us greater responsibility and more choices, but I don't think they automatically make us more happy or less happy. Many wealthy people and many intelligent people are not happy at all, and many simple people are also bitter and unhappy. I think more important than happiness are values like truth, faithfulness, and godliness. Jesus was full of joy, but He was a man of sorrows as well. The apostle Paul was full of joy, riches, life, assurance, and thankfulness, but he was burdened with many troubles. People betrayed him, he was beaten up, he was thrown in prison. Happiness was not the highest value for Paul or Jesus. I believe that the way God has made us to be, and working toward that way—embracing and confronting the struggles of a fallen world—lead to the best and fullest life but maybe not the happiest life. That's hard to accept because we want to be happy, yet happiness is only a part of reality. It's not wise to sacrifice the other parts of reality in order to be happy. Sometimes I am happy and I enjoy it very much, but happiness is not the main thing.

Do you regard Christianity as a religion?

Religion is a system of connecting with the supernatural. Christianity, as I understand it, is not primarily a system and not primarily about the supernatural. It's the reality of all things both natural and supernatural being held together by Jesus, and our living out that reality. The Pharisees in the time of Jesus were very religious—with their ceremonies, rules, special clothes, and schedules—but Jesus was unimpressed with them. He said that people's righteousness had to be greater than the Pharisees', which means the righteousness of Christians cannot be a set of regulations or a tradition or something ceremonial. It has to be a righteousness of the heart. It's a radical and personal transformation of the heart. There is nothing religious about that.

Many Christians focus excessively on going to heaven. What are your thoughts about that?

Understood correctly, what the Bible teaches is that we must work and pray so that the kingdom of God will become realized on earth. Jesus said, *Pray like this: Our Father in heaven, may Your name be known as holy, Your kingdom come, Your will be done, on earth as it is in heaven.* We recite that prayer but often we don't mean it. Sometimes what we really mean is 'my Father in heaven, please get me out of here!' That's what we have in our hearts. But that isn't what Jesus taught. He taught us to pray, and to work, that the kingdom of heaven will be on earth—that the biblical values and description of human life and relationships will be realized on earth. We're not supposed to just wait and endure it until God jerks us out of here to some other place. But I am sympathetic to the reasons why people have that attitude. We suffer, we are oppressed, we are frustrated. Still, the attitude is wrong, and we need to repent. It's partly because Christians have these wrong ideas that Christianity looks bad to non-Christians—and then we wonder why our evangelism is not very effective. Evangelism will never be effective when we preach a gospel of withdrawal and escapism.

A lot of your ideas, such as objectivity and subjectivity, dynamism, and form and freedom, are not explicitly mentioned in the Bible. Have you encountered theologians who have argued that these ideas are too abstract or speculative to be justified by the actual biblical text?

Very rarely do people make a statement that the ideas I am teaching are not biblical. More often people ask how I discern these ideas in the Bible, which is encouraging. Then I try to work with the question. An example of such a question would be, 'Why do you use the word Trinity, if it's not in the Bible?' In my understanding, the term *Trinity* is a verbal symbol for God's nature as described in the Bible. Another example of a verbal symbol is the Creeds of the Church Fathers. We call them *creeds* because they start with *credo*, or 'I believe', but the Church Fathers called them symbols and definitions because they were a representation of the whole truth in the Bible. In general, you will not find total correspondence between a symbol and the thing being symbolized. Similarly, you will not find total correspondence between verbal symbols, such as the Trinity, form and freedom, or dynamism, and the vocabulary of the Bible, even though such symbols are substantiated by the text of the Bible.

Can you say more about what it's like to be saved, and what happens afterward?

Being saved is like being remade from a dead, self-centered creature into a living, other-centered creature. To be saved is to turn from our brokenness and to begin to move in the direction of healing. That means receiving healing *and* working for healing, or as the old song goes, *trust and obey*. It's a complementarity, a 200% reality. We aren't saved by trusting God *or* obeying him, but by both. Some people get caught, thinking it's one or the other. The question *Which do you choose?* comes, I believe, directly from the devil. *Do you trust in God's healing, or work toward healing?* That's an evil question. It's like asking Humpty Dumpty which side of the wall he wants to fall on. But God says we can have both sides. Jesus says, *I have come that you might have life and have it abundantly. I am not telling you to pick the part of life you want to have. Have the whole thing. Live the whole thing.* To give another example of how we can be challenged after we're saved, consider Psalm 23. This psalm tells us, *My cup runs over.* In reality, when life *runs over* people usually react by thinking 'Oh, what a mess, let's clean this up!' People don't want things to be out of control or unpredictable. But a lack of control is unacceptable only when we walk by sight. When we walk by faith, it's acceptable because we trust in God to stabilize us in the overflowing and abundance of life. Faith can be so frightening because we are not seeing, we are not controlling, we are not totally understanding. We are walking and trusting God. It's as if you hear His voice at the end of a dark tunnel and walk toward His voice. People want to touch the walls. They want to run back and forth. They want to orient themselves. That's natural. Walking by faith is spiritual. We are drawn to the natural because we're fallen and broken. We need to turn and become spiritual. That doesn't mean to abandon the natural, but to contextualize the natural in the fullness of God's truth and reality. Some people think you've got the natural on one side and the spiritual on the other, so that you have to leave one side and come to the other when you're saved. But the biblical picture is that the natural is contextualized within the spiritual, within the Lordship of Jesus Christ. Then nothing is lost. Everything is gained. Life gets bigger and fuller.

If life gets bigger after being saved, why do we often get the opposite impression—that Christian life makes people more limited and rigid?

A question I often ask people in different countries is, 'If you went into your city and stopped ten people, and said, "I would like to ask you a question. If you would become a Christian today, do you think your life would become larger, fuller, and more engaged, or smaller, narrower, and less engaged?"—if you asked that, how would the people answer?' Generally, everyone says that the people would answer the latter; they would think that life becomes smaller, narrower, and less engaged. And I agree that that would be most people's impression. But then I ask, 'Is that what the Bible says?' They say, 'No, that isn't what the Bible says.' I agree with that, too. So where do people get the idea that becoming a Christian makes you more limited? They get it to some extent from the media and from false attacks against Christianity, but to a large degree they get it from Christians themselves. If that is the truth, then maybe the beginnings of apologetics should be an apology. Maybe we should ask people whether they can forgive us for giving them the wrong idea about what it means to live as a Christian. We also need to practice the Lordship of Jesus Christ over *all* of life, not just the religious life.

A key image of Christianity is the Crucifixion and the washing away of our sins with the blood of Christ. The image is violent, and for many people disturbing and hard to relate to. Is there any other way to convey the central message of Christianity?

Blood is it. Death is it. It can never be nice. I sometimes tell people it's like going to the dentist. A saving visit to the dentist can never be nice—not if you have a good dentist. Suppose you have a terrible toothache and the dentist says, 'Oh, you must be in awful pain. Here, let me bless you. Have some morphine.' If he then walks away and that's his solution, he hasn't blessed you, he's cursed you. To bless you is initially to *increase* the pain.

The dentist is a clear example of the painful blessing. Sometimes it can be helpful to remind people that life is not nice, and to have *more life* is not a totally nice process. Of course, people naturally prefer to imagine a nice kind of salvation. You can imagine a Buddhist or transcendental kind of thing—and a lot of people do. It's very natural and romantic to imagine a nice salvation. But the Bible doesn't give a nice salvation. It's a scandal. Paul himself says this. It's always been true. Jesus is falsely advertised as totally nice, but He isn't. He's real.

C. S. Lewis got it right in *The Lion, the Witch and the Wardrobe*. The children in the story are wondering about Aslan, a kind of symbol for Jesus, and ask, *Is he safe?* And they are told, *Of course he isn't safe. But he's good.* Safe or nice doesn't mean good. Another illustration would be a mother with her three-year-old boy about to cross the street. If the boy tries to run into a street where the cars are going back and forth, the mother's love would be expressed very violently. She would grab that little boy and jerk him off the street at risk of breaking his arm. She might shout and try to instill fear in him. And that will be her love. If, on the other hand, she had been nice, then he would have died. Our situation is urgent, and God's solution is drastic and effective.

Is God a male according to the Bible, or does He include anything of the female?

God is absolute, and from God proceed both male and female. In the Bible, we are taught to call God *Father*, but we can see in various places that He is also Mother. In the Old Testament, God says: *I would comfort you as one's own mother comforts him.* In the New Testament, Jesus says to Jerusalem that He would gather it as a mother hen gathers her chicks. We customarily call God Father in part because of His relationship with Jesus. Also, some prominent characteristics of God expressed through history demonstrate that He is powerful and law-giving—this leans in the direction of fatherhood. Still, although it would be accurate to pray to God the Father, to regard God *as a whole* as only Father would not be accurate, because God is larger than that.

What is the difference between angels and fallen angels based on your understanding?

God is three persons and other-centered. The devil is one person and self-centered. For this reason, the angels who follow God are other-centered, and the angels who follow the devil are self-centered. They are like black holes, sucking things into them. That is why the devil and fallen angels relate to people by possessing and consuming them. The angels of God, on the other hand, bless people, encourage people to be other-centered, to love, and to know the Truth.

Have Christians misread the Bible in ways that result in the misuse or exploitation of nature?

Yes. An example would be escapism eschatology. This is the belief that at the end of the world Jesus is going to come and take us away to someplace else, and burn His creation and start over in some heavenly realm. I don't believe this idea is supported by the Bible, but it has been believed by Christians and has resulted in a utilitarian attitude of 'use creation for your own purposes, because God hates it and is going to burn it up anyway.' This attitude is one of the main criticisms that New Age people and Buddhists have against Christians, and the criticism is valid.

Some would suggest the Bible is easy to misuse and misunderstand because of its complexity. Why would God create such a complex document to express His truth? Why not create something simpler?

God is complex and His image is complex. A simple expression of truth would be reductive, inadequate, and inappropriate. There is a limit on the simplicity that there can be in God's relationship to us. If it's too simple, then people will be puppets and automatons. There must be room to think and choose. God is not automatic and so His image cannot be automatic. The Bible is not unlike other things in life—marriage, for instance. Marriage is complex, and hard to understand and prone to misuse, but that doesn't mean we should get rid of it or avoid it. The fact that the Bible is complex and people misuse it deliberately or accidentally doesn't show me that the Bible is wrong. It shows me that it's realistic.

Is salvation possible for people of non-Christian religions, or for people who don't practice any religion?

Yes, not because everything is true, but because God puts eternity in the hearts of all people. We are promised that if we seek Him with all our heart, we will find Him. The reverse is also true. Many people who identify themselves as Christians are far from Christianity. You can go to a lot of churches and find people who are not Christian. You will find jealousy, pride, manipulation, greed, ecologically unsound ideas, and all sorts of problems. We are called by Jesus to be His ambassadors, and to demonstrate His reality in our relationships with each other, but we fail. That failure doesn't mean that no one can be saved. I know a lot of missionaries, and I've heard amazing stories about how people are saved without meeting a Christian. So, yes, I think that people who are without the Bible or a church, if they are honest, can know their need of God. They can become poor in spirit—the kind of people Jesus called *blessed*. If they are honest, they will cry out to God and God will answer. That's a personal, individual issue, not a religious or racial or cultural issue.

Are you saying that people can be saved without Jesus?

No, I don't mean they can be saved without Jesus, but they can be saved outside of the cultural tradition of the church. God can come to them directly. I have met people who became Christians because of a vision. I knew a missionary woman who went to Indonesia and entered a remote valley with translators. The people had never met a foreigner, and she told them, 'I have come to tell you about the Lamb of God who came to take away the sins of the world.' They said, 'We know that.' She said, 'Who told you?'

The people then recounted the story of a man, now deceased, who had been the judge of that particular tribe. The man had apparently lived in anguish for a long time because, although he was the judge of others, there was nobody to judge *him*. He couldn't live with that. He cried out, and one day he saw a vision of a lamb being slain. It was a vision of Saint John in the Apocalypse, and he understood that the Creator had died to make him just and right, and then he believed. He had never heard the word *Jesus*, but he believed in Jesus, and he taught his people to the extent of his understanding. It happens like that sometimes. That doesn't mean we don't have to tell people. We are responsible to do what we can do. But we don't need to live in despair and to think that God is cruel and unfair because of the people we cannot meet.

How can Christians connect more closely with people of the first and second circles?

That's a good question, because most people in the world are Monists or Dualists of one kind or another. If you are a Christian, there is a good chance you will have a Monist or Dualist as a neighbor. Christians know that they need to love their neighbor. To love somebody you need to understand them, because love is not a feeling. Love is a relationship with other people involving understanding, communicating, and supporting. And love is not debating and arguing. If I know everything and I win all the debates but there is no love, then it's garbage. We need to understand people in order to love them, and only then can the logic and the discussion be really valuable. It also helps to remember what Christians and non-Christians have in common. God made me a Christian, but before that He made me a human being. When I became a Christian, I did not cease to be a human being. As a Christian, there are many things I don't have in common with other people, whereas on the level of being human, there are many things I do have in common with other people. The other thing I would add is the importance of listening to people and asking deeply human questions. What does it mean to be a human being? How do we know ourselves? What is my meaning or purpose? How can I deal with my guilt? Where did everything come from and where is it going? These are the questions that everybody struggles with. Those of us who are Christians know the answer is Jesus, but *what are the questions?* That's where we need to work with people and bless people. We mustn't say to people 'I don't care what your questions are, believe in Jesus, He's the answer.' That's not love, that's just selling something. We need to ask 'What are your questions?' Then we can hopefully say 'Yes, those are my questions too! We are human. We live in a difficult world.' Then we can start exploring the answers.

You emphasize the importance of asking questions. Where in the Bible are we encouraged to ask questions or show curiosity?

God invites us to reason with Him. You see it in various places. In Isaiah 1:18 God says: *Come let us reason together.* In Genesis, God evangelizes Adam with a series of questions: *Where are you? Who told you? Have you eaten?* If this is God's evangelistic methodology, we would be wise to follow it by asking questions of each other. Also, I think asking questions is one of the reasons why Jesus wants us to be like little children. How many of you have ever known a little child that did not ask questions? Those kinds of children don't exist. It's their job to ask questions. God doesn't want us to stop thinking. He wants us to ask, to test everything—touch it, feel it, squeeze it.

Non-Christians often attend your talks. What kinds of perspectives do they bring?

I find that non-Christians often bring a fresher perspective than Christians. I think it's because non-Christians are not coming from the same cultural, traditional religious grid. Their questions are not expressed in religious jargon. They're more often expressed in common English, German, Russian, or what have you. When a Christian asks a question, they expect it to be answered within the context of the Christian worldview and traditional cultural experience, which is not the whole human reality. The Christians' questions that I get are rather predictable. Non-Christians tend to be less predictable. That gets your adrenaline going and keeps you awake. I enjoy it.

What are the unique challenges for Christians when it comes to asking questions?

I think a difficulty with born-again Christians is that they know that they are born again into the peace of God, but they think that this peace means a lack of conflict. But that isn't what the Bible means when it says *peace*. It means *shalom*, which is a foundation of well-being and understanding of reality. It's the foundation on which to have conflicts and to ask questions, and to confess to not knowing and needing to know more. Many Christians are passive and complacent in their faith, forgetting that the word *Israel* means *the one who wrestles with God*.

Doesn't asking questions provoke a sense of uncertainty and doubt, which can have the effect of weakening faith?

Asking questions makes it easier to hold on to faith in the things that the Bible wants us to believe in. If we never question in doubt, then we will never grow in understanding. The Bible wants us to believe in a personal God and a personal relationship with that God. The Bible wants us to receive people's questions, and to ask our own questions about reality. Not asking questions means our faith is weak. It means we don't trust God to sustain us in the process of crisis and confusion. There is no growth without asking questions. In verses five and seven of the fourth chapter of Proverbs, we are commanded to *get wisdom.* This means that we don't already have it. One of the ways to start getting it is by asking questions.

How does your current church community react to your questions?

Slowly but positively. Many of the questions I find in the Bible and bring to the Bible are paradigm-shifting questions. It takes most people a long time to come to grips with this kind of questioning, and it requires a lot of gentle repetition.

How can we learn to ask better questions?

There are a variety of ways. Read books that ask questions. Read novels and see films that ask questions, and think about the biblical answers. Realize that some answers aren't tied up with a bow. Think things through down to the bottom and out to the edges. Be courageous and rigorous in asking dangerous questions. Don't shy away from frightening questions. Ask questions for which you don't already have a supposed answer. Think about why the question is being asked. What difference will the answer make to your life? If your questions come out verbally garbled, try writing them down. The process is endless. You have to stay awake.

Why did you originally become a Buddhist?

I grew up in a Christian atmosphere and I kept asking absolute questions. But the Christians I knew were not interested in my questions. They said, 'Don't ask questions, just believe. Become like a little child and have faith without asking questions.' That didn't make sense to me. It was only later when I came to realize that, in telling us to become like little children, Jesus really did want us to ask and inquire and explore. As a result of my early dissatisfaction with Christianity, I began shopping around and tried out different philosophies and religions. I was in the Rosicrucian Society, the Bahai, the Self-Realization Fellowship of Paramahansa Yogananda, and other groups. I settled on Zen Buddhism because it's very unreligious. Zen Buddhists are always interested in absolutes, and I was interested in absolutes. I also appreciated the fact that they were the only religious group I knew that did not sell jewelry.

How did you become a Christian?

There are various true answers. One true answer is by free will. Another true answer is by the sovereign working of the Holy Spirit. A correct answer must include both: I choose and God chooses. In terms of the specifics of my choosing, I can think of several concrete reasons. Among the most important ones was the realization that it takes less faith to believe in Christianity than to believe in anything else. It takes more faith, in my understanding, to believe in humanism. I know people who believe that human beings are fundamentally good, and I think, wow, what faith! They believe against all the evidence! Such a powerful faith! I don't want to have a faith like that. Too much faith is destructive. I want to have a small faith in a big truth. I don't want a big faith in a wrong idea. A human being can believe anything. A human being can believe that the world is flat, and they can believe it strongly enough that they are willing to die or kill for it. But the faith that the world is flat does not make the world flat. My faith that Jesus is God and Lord does not make Him God and Lord. If He is God and Lord, then He is that independent of my believing in Him. That was important to me during my search—a truth that was independent of my faith—and the most independent understanding I found was in the biblical worldview. I also asked a lot of questions as I studied Christianity. There was a thought-loop that ran in my head for weeks. I had once sung in an English opera called *The Mikado,* and one of the lines of the opera was 'who are you who ask this question?' I kept hearing this line in my head while I was studying, and I thought, maybe I should pay attention to this. Then I thought, I am asking all these questions, but who is asking? I realized that the Buddhist answer is *Asking is,* but the Christian answer is *I am asking.* That was closer to my actual experience of myself. I had been asking questions all my life. So that was another reason why Christianity made sense to me. But I didn't struggle with things that most people do. Many people struggle with either guilt and the denial of guilt, or they struggle with the existence of the supernatural. Some are naturalists, like many scientists and engineers, who believe that if you can't measure something and express it in numbers then it doesn't exist. But I never had those difficulties. I was a supernaturalist all my life.

What difficulties did you have?

The thing that was crucial to me was the personal nature of reality. One of my questions was: Is the non-personal necessarily sub-personal? Couldn't there be a super-personal, non-personal, from which personality could proceed? To put it another way, can human reality, which is personal, result from an absolute reality that is impersonal, or can an impersonal absolute reality only result in things that are less than personal? That was a very serious question for me, and it was very difficult to find a Christian who would take it seriously, or who could even begin to understand what the question was. The Buddhist answer to the question is *Yes*—an impersonal absolute realty can give rise to a personal human reality in the illusion of diversity—but the Christian answer is *No*—only a personal absolute reality can create a personal human reality. I wanted to know why Christians believed in their answer, and why the Buddhist answer might not be right. The Lord had to guide me to the L'Abri Fellowship in Switzerland before I could even find people who could understand my questions and help me. But that was my own unique struggle. We are each different. I can tell you how and why I came to be a Christian, but you cannot do it that way. You have to do it your own way. You are not me. You are unique. You have to come to God and God has to come to you in a way that you understand intellectually, emotionally, existentially, and morally, in ways that I might not understand. According to the Bible, your relationship to God is like a marriage. Christians often speak of sharing their faith, but I don't believe I can share my faith. I think I can share *the* faith—what is believed by Christians—but I cannot share *my* faith any more than I can share my marriage. I have a marriage, and I can tell you about it, but I cannot share it with you. I have a faith in Jesus Christ, and I can tell you about it, but I cannot share it with you. You have to have your own. You cannot have it by copying another person, or by inheriting it from your parents or your grandparents.

We can say that God has no grandchildren. He only has children. Each one has to come directly to Him.

Given that you're the kind of person who continues to ask questions about worldviews, do you think it's possible that you might one day find a different answer and abandon Christianity?

I want to be careful that my Christianity doesn't become fanaticism, or something that I believe because I believe. If someone proved that they'd found the bones of Jesus, I would cease to be a Christian at that moment, because it wouldn't be true. There are parts about being a Christian that I enjoy, but I would sacrifice those for truth. I think you have to stay open, but at the same time faithful and committed. You might meet a lot of interesting women, but you should only marry one of them. That means you need to say *No* to many women and *Yes* to just one. The relationship with Jesus, as I've already mentioned, is like a marriage. If you would discover that the woman you married has serious problems and was married eight times before and has nine children that you didn't know about, then you might leave that situation. In a similar way, if I discovered that Jesus was a lie, then I would go through a fundamental crisis. And as far as I can imagine now, I would go back to Zen Buddhism. But the falsity of Christianity would have to be really established in various ways for me to give up my faith in it.

Do you still encounter people in the church now who tell you 'don't ask, just believe'?

Much less—partly because I am older and people want to be polite, and partly because I now pastor in a church where many of the people do scientific research. Their entire careers are about asking questions.

I find it interesting, however, that many Christians who are scientists and researchers will separate their scientific work from their religious faith. They will say 'this is faith but that is knowledge.' That's schizophrenic. I don't think it's healthy. It's so common probably because to compartmentalize is to simplify and to have control, and people feel good about doing that. But I'm always encouraging people to put things together. Everything belongs together in Jesus. When you read the Bible, you should not only ask 'Do I believe it?' but also 'What does it mean?' You never finish finding out. You have to stay awake. You have to stay as a little child.

Your attitude of openness and curiosity is unusual for a pastor. Does that reflect your years of practice as a Buddhist?

I don't know. There are certainly some things I have retained from my Zen Buddhist background that are good. They are not things you can't find in the Bible, but they are things that Christians have not emphasized much. The main one is the idea of the importance of the ordinary. In Zen, the ordinary things are special and the special things are ordinary. I think that's biblical, although Christians themselves have tended to ignore the ordinary and value the special things, the special experiences, the special places, the special holy hardware. In Ecclesiastes we are encouraged to dig in the garden and eat and be thankful to God. It's very ordinary. The Zen emphasis on the ordinary also includes valuing creation. Zen Buddhists don't know that God created it, but they value it. One of the great sayings of Zen is: *Buddha is a manure pile.* This means that if you don't recognize Buddha in the manure pile when you're shoveling in the garden, then you don't know Buddha. As a result, Zen Buddhists tend not to exploit or abandon nature. They try to incorporate nature into Buddha-nature. The Bible gives us responsibility to take care of the creation that God loves, but Christians sometimes stray from that.

Do you have a denominational preference?

My own personal practice has Baptist and Brethren tendencies. I can, however, see great value in liturgy. I certainly enjoy it. I see value in the systematic living out of God's salvific history and His word through symbol and text and activity, rather than through a haphazard 'as the occasion arises' or 'as the mood strikes' sort of approach. At the same time, there are dangers that we may begin to worship the tradition of the liturgy itself. Also, many people who are in liturgical churches have very little idea of what any of it means. They do it because it's done. They may practice it for a sense of belonging, or social advantage, or out of habit. Someone once referred to liturgy as *truth hidden by many sacred veils*. I think that may be the case for many people.

Do you experience life's pain as less painful because you are a Christian?

No. It's more hopeful, but I don't experience less pain. There may be *more* pain, in fact. The pain of a Christian is not only their own pain, but the pain of the world, the pain that Christ feels for humanity—not that I am particularly acute in this sensitivity compared to others. Still, I think that in the Christian life, as people walk the walk and run the race, one becomes more sensitive rather than less sensitive. Life becomes more intense, richer, fuller, with more pain and more joy.

What is one of the most important answers you have received from the Bible?

The fourth chapter of Philippians is very precious to me. Paul tells us not to be anxious about anything, but in everything, in all the circumstances and details of your life, by prayer and supplication, bring your requests to God. Don't hide anything from God. Bring everything. Tell Him your point of view. Tell Him what you want. You're not God, you don't see perfectly, but tell Him what you want. Find out how you see things and what you think a good way would be and then tell God. Now, if you do this, the promise is pointedly *not* that God will give you what you ask for. That would be a terrible curse. One of the worst wishes you can have for another person is 'may you get what you want.' They'll surely be destroyed. So God doesn't say He'll give us what we want. The promise is that He will *keep* us. *The peace of God, which passes all understanding, will keep your hearts and minds through Jesus Christ.* That is the promise. What are the details of the outworking of that promise? They are infinite. We don't know what that promise-keeping will look like from one person to the next or from one circumstance to the next. We don't know the details. We know only the security that God will keep us and never let us go. So, when we experience situations that are painful, infuriating, confusing, uncomfortable, threatening, and we wonder, does God keep me . . . ?

We can be sure that the answer is always YES.

Portrait of the author by Andrzej Bednarczyk, professor of painting at Akademia Sztuk Pieknych in Krakow, Poland, sketched during a lecture in Kazimierz in 1991.

Profound thanks to:

Peco Gaskovski
our editor, who gave my written
voice shape, order, and color by his
rich gifts and tremendous labor.

Katharine Wolff
our designer, who showed me what
makes a book beautiful and how
it is done.

Ralph McCall
our publisher, who oversaw the
production process and guided me
through it.

Marsh Moyle
whose discerning reading of the
first draft prompted some important
changes.

Lillian Myers
who first edited and published much
of this material in article form.

Ruth Gaskovski
who transcribed and proofread and
suggested and encouraged.

Destinée Media aims to bring a fresh perspective to living, culture, and worldviews. This is the first book of a series based on the lectures of Ellis Potter.

www.ingramcontent.com/pod-product-compliance
Lightning Source LLC
Chambersburg PA
CBHW030332230426
43661CB00032B/1378/J